Henry David Thoreau

헨리 데이비드 소로

Biography Comic
who? ㉓ Henry David Thoreau

초판 1쇄 인쇄 2011년 4월 8일
초판 2쇄 발행 2013년 7월 5일

지은이 오영석
그린이 스튜디오 청비
번역 자넷 재완 신
감수 김수희
펴낸이 김선식

Chief Story Creator 김정미
Story Creator 채정은
Design Creator 김경민
Marketing Creator 신문수

4th Creative Story Team 김선영, 이유미, 김선민, 전해인, 최수아
Creative Design Dept. 박효영
Creative Management Team 김성자, 송현주, 권송이, 김민아, 윤이경, 한선미
Creative Marketing Dept. 최창규, 이주화, 이상혁, 박현미, 백미숙
　　　　Communication Team 서선행
　　　　Contents Rights Team 김미영

펴낸곳 (주)다산북스
주소 서울시 마포구 서교동 395-27번지
전화 02-702-1724(기획편집) 02-703-1725(마케팅) 02-704-1724(경영지원)
팩스 02-703-2219
이메일 dasanbooks@hanmail.net
홈페이지 www.dasanbooks.com
출판등록 2005년 12월 23일 제313-2005-00277호

필름 출력 스크린그래픽센타　**종이** 월드페이퍼(주)　**인쇄 · 제본** (주)현문

ISBN　978-89-6370-451-7　14740
SET　　978-89-6370-438-8

who?

Henry David Thoreau

헨리 데이비드 소로

글 **오영석** | 그림 **스튜디오 청비** | 번역 **채드 워커** | 감수 **김수희**

Dasan Kid

Henry David Thoreau

Poet, Philosopher, July 12, 1817 ~ May 6, 1862

The philosopher who praised simple living in harmony with nature, Henry David Thoreau was born by the Concord River in the U.S. state of Massachusetts in 1817. The beautiful Concord River and the woods nearby were Henry's closest playground as well as teacher.

After he graduated school, Thoreau became a teacher. He opposed the strict education and physical punishment that was in place at the time, and preferred to befriend his students instead. However, his fellow teachers did not approve of his teaching style and Thoreau was eventually fired.

He wanted to pass on to students what he had learned from nature, so he and his brother John established their own school. Instead of having students memorize books and writing, they wanted students to learn by experiencing for themselves and becoming intimate with the subject. Their students liked this teaching method, which pleased Thoreau. Then while traveling along the Concord River during vacation, Thoreau's brother suddenly became ill and died. Thoreau, in turn, lost all motivation and closed down the school.

After this tragedy, Thoreau built his own house by a beautiful pond called Walden Pond and began to write. At Walden, he used only what he needed from nature, living a simple life without waste, and wrote down everything he did there. Two years later, he left Walden and published his writings in a book.

After he returned to society, he was arrested for evading taxes while living on Walden Pond. From this experience, Thoreau wrote a book called Civil Disobedience, which stated that a citizen has the right not to pay taxes if the government is doing something he/she does not approve of.

While in his forties, Thoreau's health took a turn for the worse, and at the young age of forty-five, he returned to be with nature eternally. His book did not get much attention at the time it was published, but it is now considered a great work which is continually mentioned whenever people these days talk about the relationship between nature and man.

헨리 데이비드 소로

시인이자 사상가, 1817년 7월 12일 ~ 1862년 5월 6일

자연과 어울려 사는 소박한 삶을 찬양했던 철학자 헨리 데이비드 소로는 1817년, 미국 매사추세츠 콩코드 강가에서 태어났습니다. 아름다운 강과 숲이 있었던 콩코드 강가는 어린 소로에게 가장 가까운 놀이터이자 선생님이었습니다.

학교를 졸업한 소로는 선생님으로 일하게 되었습니다. 소로는 당시 보편적으로 시행되던 엄격한 교육과 체벌을 반대하며, 학생들과 친구처럼 지내고 싶어 했습니다. 그러나 다른 선생님들은 그의 교육 방식에 반대하였고, 결국 소로는 해고되고 맙니다.

자신이 자연에서 배운 것들을 아이들에게 전하려 했던 소로는 형 존과 함께 학교를 세웁니다. 그곳에서 그는 책이나 글로 외워서 하는 공부보다 몸으로 체험하며 깊이 느낄 수 있는 교육을 합니다. 학생들은 소로의 교육법을 좋아하였고, 소로도 큰 보람을 느꼈습니다. 그러나 방학을 이용해 떠난 콩코드 강 여행에서 형이 병을 얻어 죽게 되자, 모든 의욕을 잃고 학교를 닫습니다.

이후 소로는 월든이라는 아름다운 호숫가에 스스로 집을 짓고 살며 글을 쓰기 시작합니다. 그곳에서 그는 자신이 꼭 필요한 만큼만 자연을 이용하고, 낭비하지 않는 소박한 삶을 살며, 모든 것을 기록으로 남깁니다. 그리고 2년 후, 월든 호수에서 나와 그 글들을 모아 책으로 냅니다.

한편, 월든 호수에서 혼자 생활하는 동안 세금을 내지 않았다는 이유로 소로는 감옥에 갇히게 됩니다. 그는 이 경험을 바탕으로 '시민은 원치 정부가 원치 않는 일을 할 때 세금을 내지 않을 권리가 있다'는 내용의 책 '시민 불복종'을 냅니다.

40대가 되어 급격히 건강이 나빠진 소로는 45세의 젊은 나이에 영원히 자연으로 돌아갔습니다. 그의 책은 당시에는 좋은 반응을 얻지 못했지만, 현대에 들어 자연과 인간의 관계를 이야기할 때 끊임없이 재해석되는 훌륭한 작품으로 남았습니다.

글 · 오영석

어린이들이 재미있고 신나게 읽을 수 있는 책을 쓰기 위해 노력하는 작가입니다. 나와 똑같이 고민하고, 실패했던 위인들의 이야기를 통해 독자들도 '할 수 있다'는 마음을 가지길 바랍니다. 작품으로『세계사 한국사』,『과학 교과 주제 탐구Q. 몸』,『걸어서 세계 속으로 2. 일본』등이 있습니다.

그림 · 스튜디오 청비

기발한 상상력을 바탕으로 새롭고 재미있는 콘텐츠를 만들어 내는 만화 창작 집단입니다. 어린이들이 책을 읽고 큰 꿈을 품기를 바라는 마음으로 즐겁게 작업하고 있습니다. 작품으로『성철 스님』,『아 다르고 어 다른 우리말 101가지』,『반기문 유엔 사무총장의 꿈과 도전』등이 있습니다.

번역 · 채드 워커(Chad Walker)

미국 텍사스 오스틴에서 심리학과 일본어를 전공했습니다. 일본으로 건너가 10년 간 살았고 이후 한국과 중국을 오가며 한 · 중 · 일의 동아시아 문화를 비교 연구하고 있습니다. 현재는 연세대학교 국어국문학과 박사 과정 중에 있습니다. 옮긴 책으로『한국어 교육을 위한 한국어 연어사전』,『한국인의 가치 문화』,『속성 한국어』등이 있습니다.

감수 · 김수희

연세대학교에서 역사를 전공했습니다. 이후 한국뿐 아니라 일본, 미국에서 한국어, 일본어, 영어를 가르쳐 왔으며 부모를 위한 영어교육용 책을 썼습니다. 영어교육채널 EBSe '엄마표 영어특강'에서 강의를 하며 홈스쿨, 알파벳과 파닉스, 다차원 테마 영어 수업 기법을 알리고 있습니다. 전국 각지에서 어린이 영어 교육에 대한 강연을 하며 창의적이고 열정적인 교수법으로 영어를 배우고자 하는 어린이와 부모들에게 많은 도움을 주고 있습니다.

Henry David Thoreau
How much did it cost for Henry David Thoreau to build his cabin at Walden Pond?

a. About 28 dollars
b. About 120 dollars
c. About 513 dollars

Answer: a

Contents

01   A Special Boy from Concord

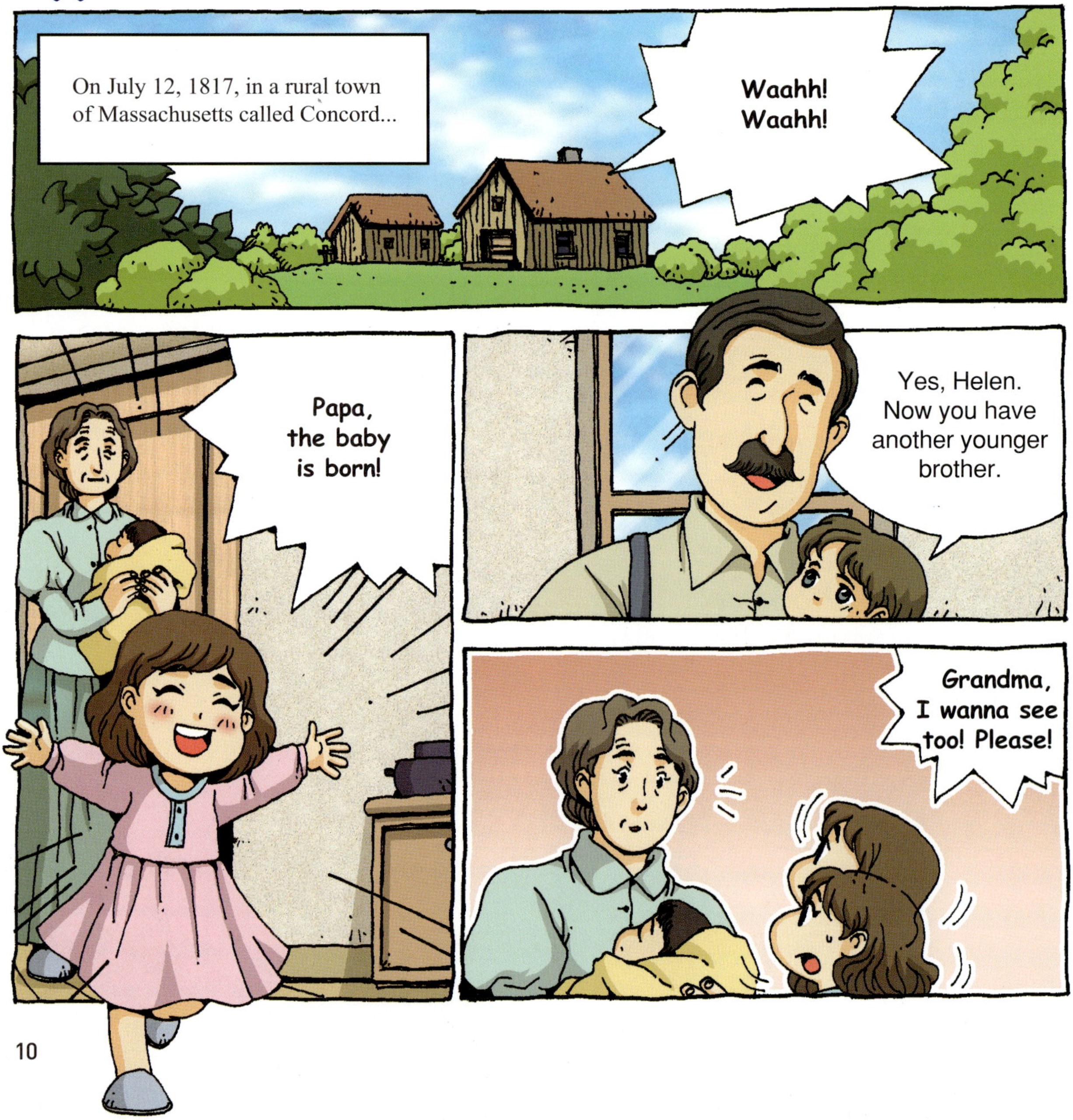

Of course. Isn't he adorable?
Hello. I'm your sister.
What a calm baby. He doesn't even cry.

Haha. He seems to be born with the tranquility of Concord.
I'll name him Henry David.

As Henry grew up, he continued to be a quiet boy.
Ow!
Yay!
Oh no, are you hurt? You've got to be careful.
Haha. Those boys get so excited over nothing.

Isn't that the pencil factory owner's child? Why doesn't he play with the other kids?
Henry's a little peculiar. He doesn't play with his peers.
Unlike his peers, Henry preferred to be by himself rather than play with friends. Adults considered him a strange child.
Henry was different from the other children, and they didn't like him very much.
Why doesn't that kid ever play with us?
He doesn't go to church and he didn't even go to the town festival.

Even after he started attending school, Henry didn't change. Then one day...
What should we do after school?
Yesterday, our duck's eggs hatched...
Huh? Where did it go?
What happened?
My pocket knife is gone.

The knife your father bought for you?

I know I put it in here...

I saw you put it there yesterday.
Hmmm...

Doesn't he look suspicious?

Who?

Henry's poor. Plus, he's always alone in the classroom.

Then, then are you saying that Henry stole my pocket knife?

Hold on. I'll go find out.

Henry, you stole the pocket knife, didn't you?
I didn't take it.

Liar! Before I start looking through your bag, tell me the truth!

Do whatever you want. Now, will you please move your hand so I can read?

What?

That's strange. It's not here.
He could've hidden it somewhere else.
The other kids suspected Henry and searched his bag thoroughly. However, Henry just continued to read his book without a word.
Several days passed.
Uh, Henry.
Yeah?
I found the kid who stole my pocket knife. Sorry for doubting you all this time.
Really? That's good. Don't worry about it.
You're alright? Don't you ever get angry? Why didn't you try to defend yourself?
I told you I didn't take your knife.
Uh, okay.

Henry possessed a composure that somehow did not befit a child. He didn't run around and play like the other children, nor did he talk much. He appeared to the other children like a solemn judge, so 'Judge' became Henry's nickname.
There goes the Judge.
What in the world does he do all day at home?
He probably just reads.
I'm home.

*abolitionists: People who advocate getting rid of the system of slavery and giving slaves their freedom and rights.

Henry's father ran a pencil factory, but he used to be a teacher. He was a learned man and had an open mind.

Oppressing another person because of the fact that his skin color is different is something that should not happen.

Henry's mother was an energetic woman with a warm heart.

That's right. If you all ever need a place to meet to discuss abolition issues, you can meet at our house anytime.

So why are they meeting?

It's for blacks' freedom.

Freedom?

I don't know exactly either. What adults talk about is always so complicated.

Hoho. Alright, we'll see you again soon.
Thank you for opening up your home, Mr. and Mrs. Thoreau.
Kids, you can come in now.
Yes, Mother. I'll get Henry and Sophia.
There were six members in Henry's family: Henry's quiet, introverted father, his outgoing mother, his mature older sister Helen, his cheerful older brother John, Henry, and his younger sister Sophia, who was two years younger than him.

From now on, we're going to have an abolitionist meeting at our house about once a week.

What are those meetings for?

There are some basic things that people need in order to live like a human being, things like the right to work where you want to work and the right to move about freely.

Unfortunately, slaves have been deprived of all these basic rights.

Do we have the basic things that people need in order to live like a human being?

Of course. If we think about it, we're rich.

We have much more than the basics that we need to live.

After hearing what his parents said, Henry had a lot to think about.
The phrase, "the basic things that people need in order to live like a human being," in particular left a deep impression on him.
Oh, that's right. We've all been invited to Mr. Stevens' house. You'll all go, won't you?
You mean, the richest man in town, Mr. Stevens?
Hoho. Yes. There will be a lot of good food there.

Is it okay
if I don't go?
You don't
want to go?
There's a book that
I want to finish. I just
want to stay at home.
That's fine.
If that's what you
want, go ahead.
That's your choice.
Thanks,
Mother.

Henry was a child who had the courage to say 'no' to things that he didn't want to do. As a result, he didn't go to the town festival that everyone went to, and he would deny an invitation to a wealthy man's house.

But his parents did not consider their son's behavior unusual at all.

Their liberal thinking, which allowed them as whites to gladly open up their home to black abolitionists, also applied to their son.

Henry and his siblings were influenced by their parents' mindset. They were able to express their opinions confidently and they respected one another's thoughts.

That's good, Henry. I was thinking about not going, either. Let's read together.

Yeah, okay!

02 Together with John

Track 09 ▶

Although Henry was a quiet boy, he would get excited and energetic with his brother, John. The two boys liked to pretend to be legendary Indian heroes of Concord.

Hmm, that's too bad. I should've gathered more weapons!
Weapons?
Like this.
Concord, Henry's hometown, was a gift of land that the Indians had given to the white settlers during the era when the New World was just being settled. As a result, there were traces of the Indians' presence and their legends preserved in the forest.
They say this is where the Indians used to live a long time ago.
Indians?
Yeah. I heard about it a while ago. The Indians built mud huts here...
...and built fires to cook with.

Wow...
What did the Indians eat?
They mostly ate flowers and fruits picked from trees.
And they also hunted fish and forest animals.

That's so neat!
I want to live
like them!
Who lives like
that these
days? That's
impossible.
Impossible?
Why not?
Indians were
people just
like us.

Henry, let's go that way. Let's run like Indians.
Okay! This time, I'm gonna win.

Hahaha. I'm faster than you!

Henry, watch out! There's a cliff!

John, hurry up! It feels great here!
Huh?
Live in harmony with nature.

Huff huff. You can't just run in any random direction like that! It's dangerous.
Huh? What's wrong?
John, I feel so good. Do you think the birds or deer living in the forest feel like this?
Maybe. I haven't run like that in a long time. It feels good.
Ahhhh!

I want to live
as free as a bird.
Yuck!
What is
this?
Hahaha!
It's bird poop!

Track 14 ▶

Henry and John's favorite places were the woods behind town and the North Bridge on the Concord River. North Bridge was one of the historical sites where the battles of the American Revolutionary War took place.

Wash your face well, Henry.

I'm all done. Do you want to smell? Heh heh.

Ugh. No thanks.

Did you know that a long time ago there used to be a wooden bridge here?

Yeah, but British soldiers set it on fire.

Yeah, that's right!

During the period of British rule over the American colonies, the Revolutionary War broke out when America wanted to gain independence from Britain. The North Bridge in Concord was a location of one of the battles of the Revolutionary War.
You evil people. This is a colony of the British Empire! Surrender immediately and be ready for the judgment of the King of England.
We are going to be free! This land is no longer a colony of England. We are Americans and we are going to win our freedom from England!
You need more than just words! Attack them!
Defense! Stand up against the British soldiers and fight!

In the woods and the North Bridge, Henry and John would sometimes pretend to be Indians and sometimes Revolutionary War soldiers. That's how the brothers became familiar with history and nature.

Several years later, Henry and John entered Concord Academy, an upper school.

Let's look at page 37 in your textbook. What we have to know here is...

School is a really boring place.

Why? You don't like your classes?

Honestly, I think I can learn more in the woods than I do at school.

How?

At school, we just memorize what's written in the books. How can we learn about a flower without touching it or smelling it?

That's true. I don't like being stuck in the classroom, either.
I miss the woods where everything lives and breathes. I miss North Bridge, too.

Henry wasn't enjoying his school classes. The more he felt this way, the more he missed the woods where he could freely run around and play.

What are you doing, Henry?

Are you waiting for John?

Oh hey, Sophia. I was just looking at the woods.

The woods? But you see them every day. What's so new about them?

I wish I could be there in the woods.

If you want to, all you have to do is go.

Huh?

that's right. It's so simple.
Thanks, Sophia!
Hahaha! I'll be back soon!
Henry headed for the forest. Everything was just the way it was when he was a child—the fresh breeze, the birds flying in between the trees.
Woohoo! This is it!
Ahh. So refreshing!
But... have I gone too far?

Where am I? It's so dark I can't see anything.

RUSTLE!

What is it? Could it be... a wolf?

Ahhhh!

Whew. It was just a cricket. You little critter, where did you...

Henry happened to stumble upon a beautiful pond in the forest. About two kilometers from Concord was Walden Pond.

Wow!

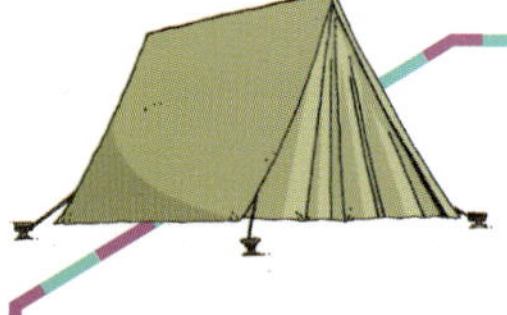

Meeting Ralph Waldo Emerson

Henry often visited Walden Pond. He went there to enjoy nature by going fishing by boat or swimming. Some days, he would do nothing but stare into the pond.

But he couldn't live in the woods or by the pond forever. Henry graduated high school, entered Harvard University, and began college life.

What Henry did most in college was to read in the library. He spent most of his four years in college with books.

Henry David Thoreau?

Huh? Me?

I'm Charles Wheeler. I'm in one of your classes.
Oh, really?
People were right. All I have to do is go to the library if I want to find you.
That's true. So what do you want?
I was just curious to see what kind of person the talk of the school was. I want to be friends.
What are you reading?
Nature.

*Emerson: Ralph Waldo Emerson (1803-1882). An American philosopher of idealism.

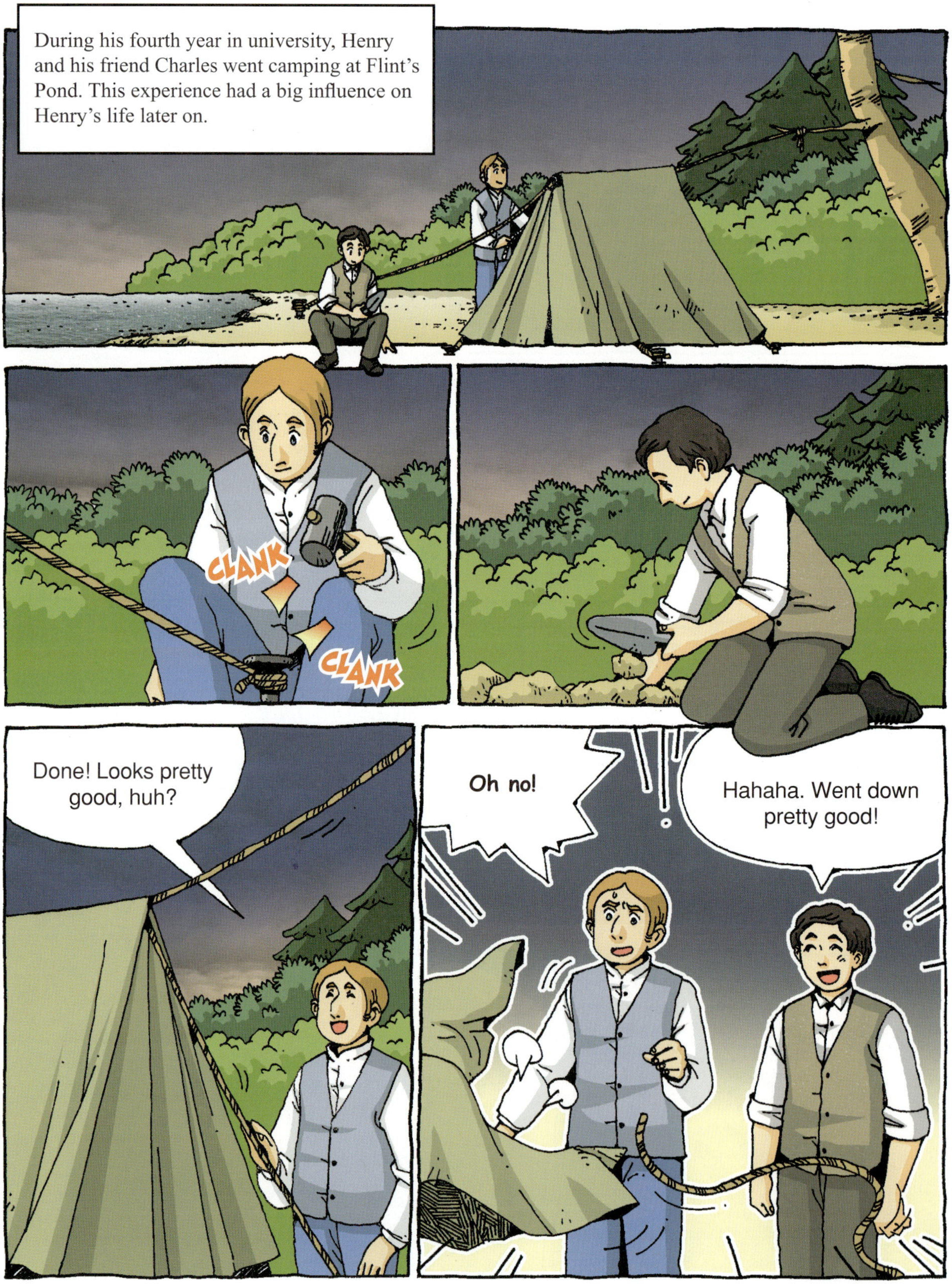

During his fourth year in university, Henry and his friend Charles went camping at Flint's Pond. This experience had a big influence on Henry's life later on.

If we just leave it like this, the pot's going to be too hot to hold.
Right. What should we do?
How about this? Let's pile rocks on each side of the campfire and...
...hang the pot from there.
It's a pot barbeque!
Hahaha.

All of the experiences, from pitching the tent by himself to cooking to finding a place to sleep, got Henry excited. He recorded these happy moments in a journal.

This existence, indeed, of living together with nature is the true form of man. The truth gained from experiencing real life is more precious than some profound words in a book. Today I existed in nature in the form of the most natural man.

During school vacation, Henry went back to his home in the country.
Long time no see, Henry.
How have you been, Sophia?
What is all that?
Just some things I wrote in my spare time.
Wow, can I see?
Sure.
Not long afterwards, Henry's sister, Sophia, encounters something uncanny at the lecture of a popular philosopher of the time, Ralph Waldo Emerson.
Ladies and gentlemen, what you understand with your mind from books is knowledge, not truth. Truth is what you realize as you experience something. In order for us to obtain truth, we must get rid of all selfishness and greed, and return to the true form of man in nature.

Sophia passed on her brother's writing to Ralph Waldo Emerson through a good friend she knew.

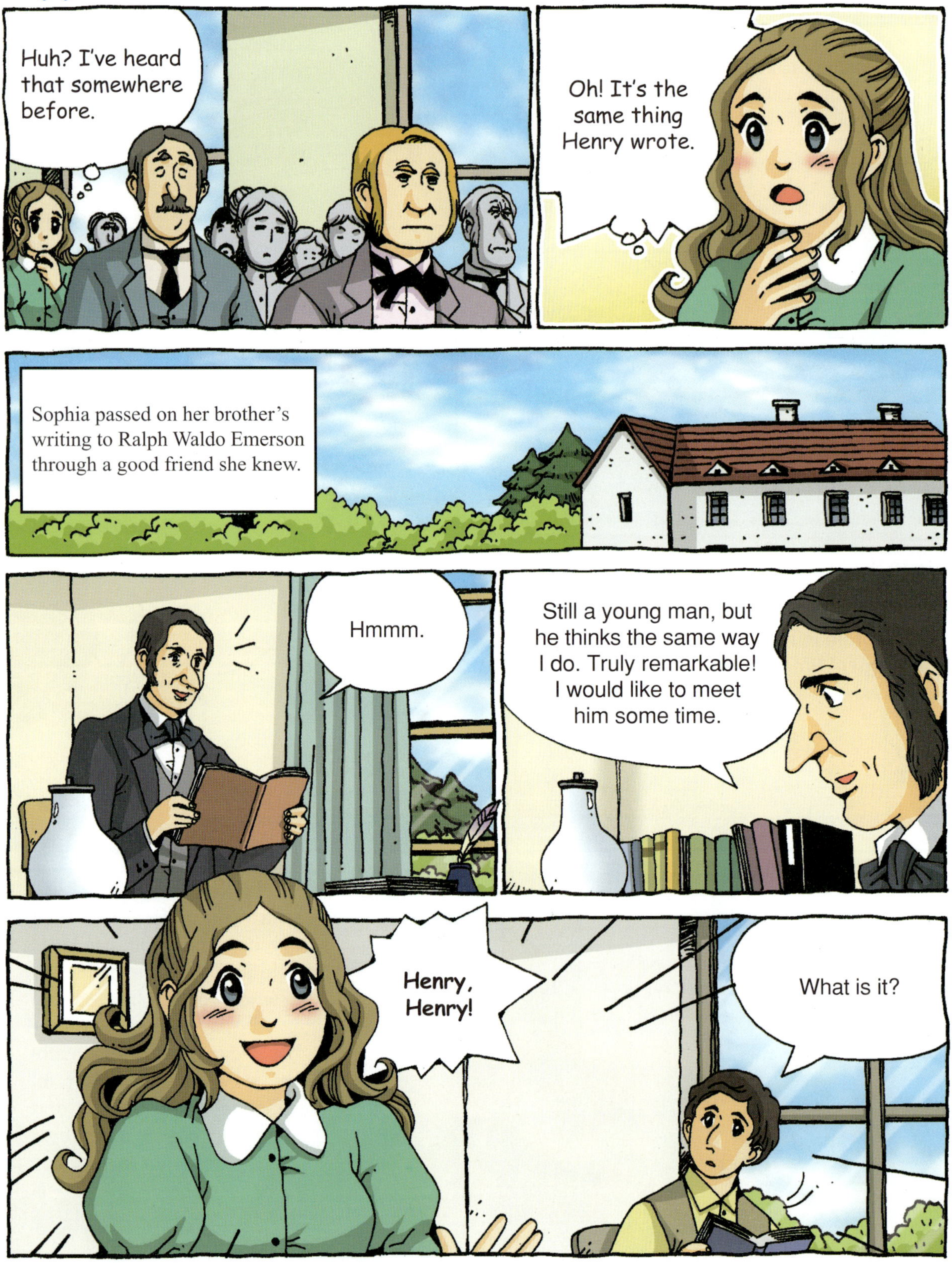

A few days later, Henry visited Emerson's home. As soon as Emerson saw Henry's animated eyes, he could see that he was not an ordinary young man.

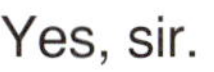

That's correct.
Therefore, instead of desiring fame or wealth in this world, we need to find truth in nature and life.
I believe that as well. When a person is one with nature, he is closest to the truth.
If a person doesn't want his true self robbed by things like religion or fame or money, he must return to nature, to the true state of man.
Haha. Keep talking. I think you and I will get along just fine.
I think so too, Mr. Emerson.

Henry and Emerson talked for a long time. Despite their age difference of 14 years, they began a friendship of two people whose thoughts were perfectly in sync with one another.

Later, Emerson would introduce Henry to the Concord Group, a gathering of transcendentalists. Through this gathering, Henry would become close with young philosophers such as Alcott, Parker, and Hedge, and would refine his own thinking and philosophy.

Becoming a Teacher

Track 25 ▶

Ahhh, I won't do it again.
Even though he himself was a teacher, Henry did not believe in using physical force to teach someone. He believed that everyone was equal and had the right to act freely.
Corporal punishment is not ethical. That's merely using one's rank to restrict someone else's freedom by force.

Punishment
Rod
Hmm.

Huh? Why is he grabbing the stick as soon as he walks in here?
I don't know. He must be a really strict teacher.
I want to make a promise to you all. I will not be using this stick.
Corporal punishment is an act which takes away one of the most basic rights of a human being. It is an inhumane method to easily exert control, which suppresses a person's individuality.

Is he serious?
No way.

Henry kept his promise not to hit his students. But one day...
Mr. Thoreau.
Yes, sir.
I heard that you don't use corporal punishment even when your students misbehave. Is that true?
There are no students who misbehave enough to get hit.
Really? But other teachers are complaining because you are the only one not using corporal punishment. I hope, Mr. Thoreau, that you will change your ways.

I'll be keeping watch.
I will not change my ways, sir.
It was one Sunday morning.
DING
DING
DING
Boy, those church bells are so loud.
Henry, you're not going to church? We got a letter inviting us to Dr. Ripley's religious meeting.

Dr. Ripley? Then it's probably a meeting to get us to give money to the clergy.
Well, it said it was mandatory for all teachers.
I'm not going. Why do all of the teachers have to support the clergy?
Well, the clergy are also teachers in a way. They teach God's Word and truth, right?
It makes sense for teachers to help people who are doing a similar work.
Clergymen and teachers are different. Teachers teach what is essential to know in life, but pastors only teach about God's Word.
Do you remember Mother and Father's words? Everyone has the freedom to choose. I don't want to be someone who blindly follows the teachings of the church. I'm going to find the right direction on my own.

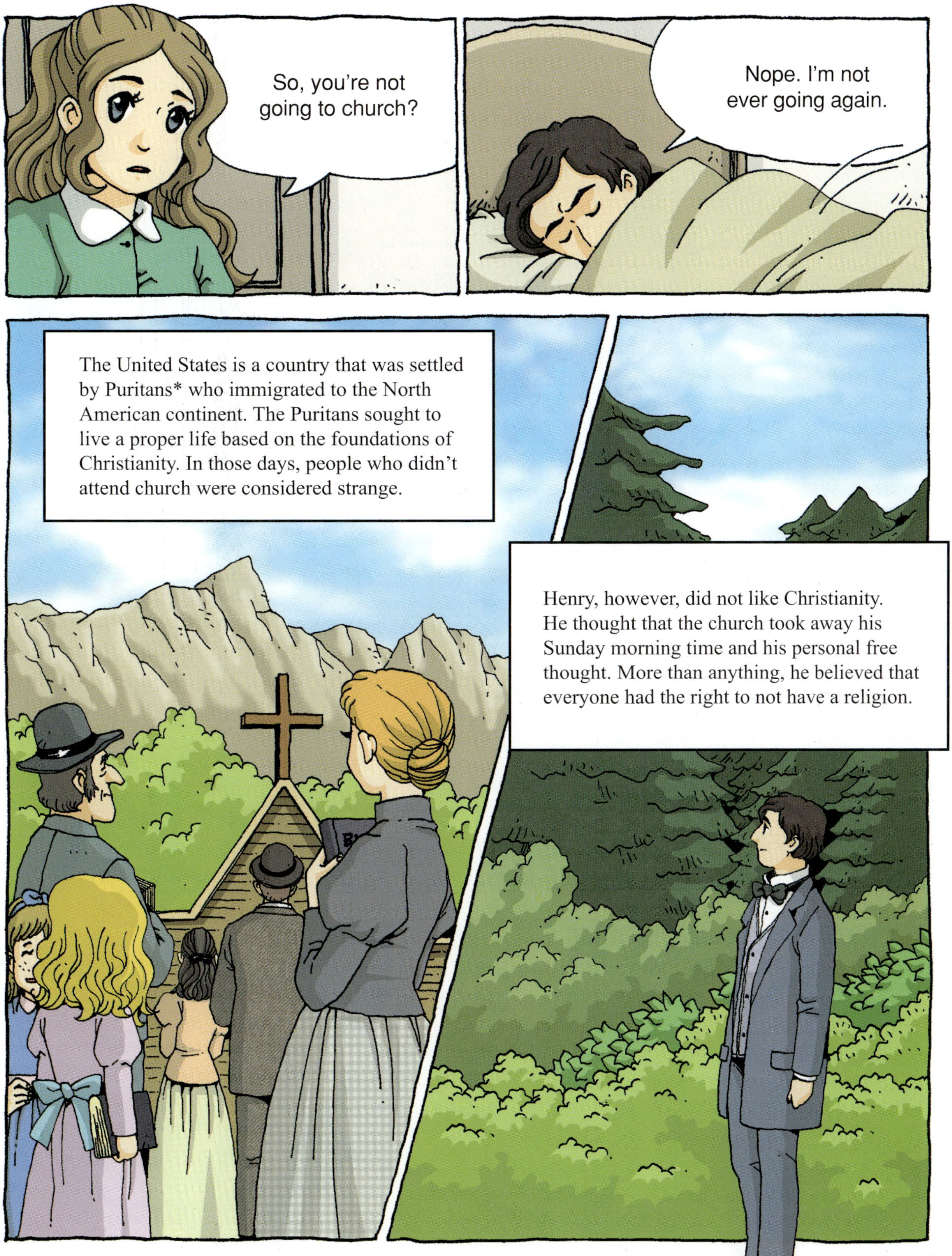

The United States is a country that was settled by Puritans* who immigrated to the North American continent. The Puritans sought to live a proper life based on the foundations of Christianity. In those days, people who didn't attend church were considered strange.

Henry, however, did not like Christianity. He thought that the church took away his Sunday morning time and his personal free thought. More than anything, he believed that everyone had the right to not have a religion.

*Puritans: One Protestant sect which formed in opposition to the Church of England in the late 16th century.

Truth is not something that is in the Bible or the church. It's in what I can touch and feel in this world.

Henry did not attend the clergy support meeting which was mandatory for teachers, and he refused to give any money to the church.

DING
DING
DING

Mr. Thoreau! Why didn't you attend yesterday's meeting?

Excuse me?

I will not put up with this anymore! We will determine at today's general meeting who is exactly at fault!

It is impossible to hold a proper class without using physical discipline. The students have gotten spoiled because of Mr. Thoreau.
That is not true. Teaching can indeed be done without using physical discipline. Corporal punishment is merely a means to control students using coercion.
Ha, sounds impressive. But school is a social organization. In order to maintain social order, there needs to be personal sacrifice!
Excuse me? Whose idea is it that individuals have to sacrifice for the sake of the group? It is possible to have a case in which citizens are right and the government is wrong. In the same way, students may be right and the school may be wrong.

What? Are you trying to say that all of us are teaching incorrectly?
We have been teaching far longer than you have. You'd best be careful what you say.

I-I didn't mean that...

On top of this, you excused yourself from attending the Ripley religious meeting a while back, didn't you? And you don't attend church at all. Your faith and your ethics are questionable.

Not going to church has nothing to do with my ethics. Having a religion or not having one is one's personal freedom.
I believe more than anything that what a person thinks is what is important. However, the church of today forces everyone to think and act the same way.

Ahem, that is a dangerous thought. You dare to reject the church. It's this kind of person that breaks the rules and doesn't use corporal punishment.
Mr. Thoreau, get rid of your useless stubbornness and discipline your students! That is real education.
If you don't, we will take that to be an act of defiance against us.
Disciplining students is real education?
If you don't want to defy us, promise us this, that you are going to use the punishment stick!
I... promise.

A few days later, many of the teachers came into Henry's classroom. They wanted to verify whether Henry was really using corporal punishment.

Alright, let's read. Everyone, turn to page 56 in the textbook.

Jack, did you forget your book?

Yes, sir. I'm sorry.

Sigh.

Jack, bring me the punishment stick.

Excuse me?

Bring the punishment stick.

Here,
here it is.

Hold out
your hands.

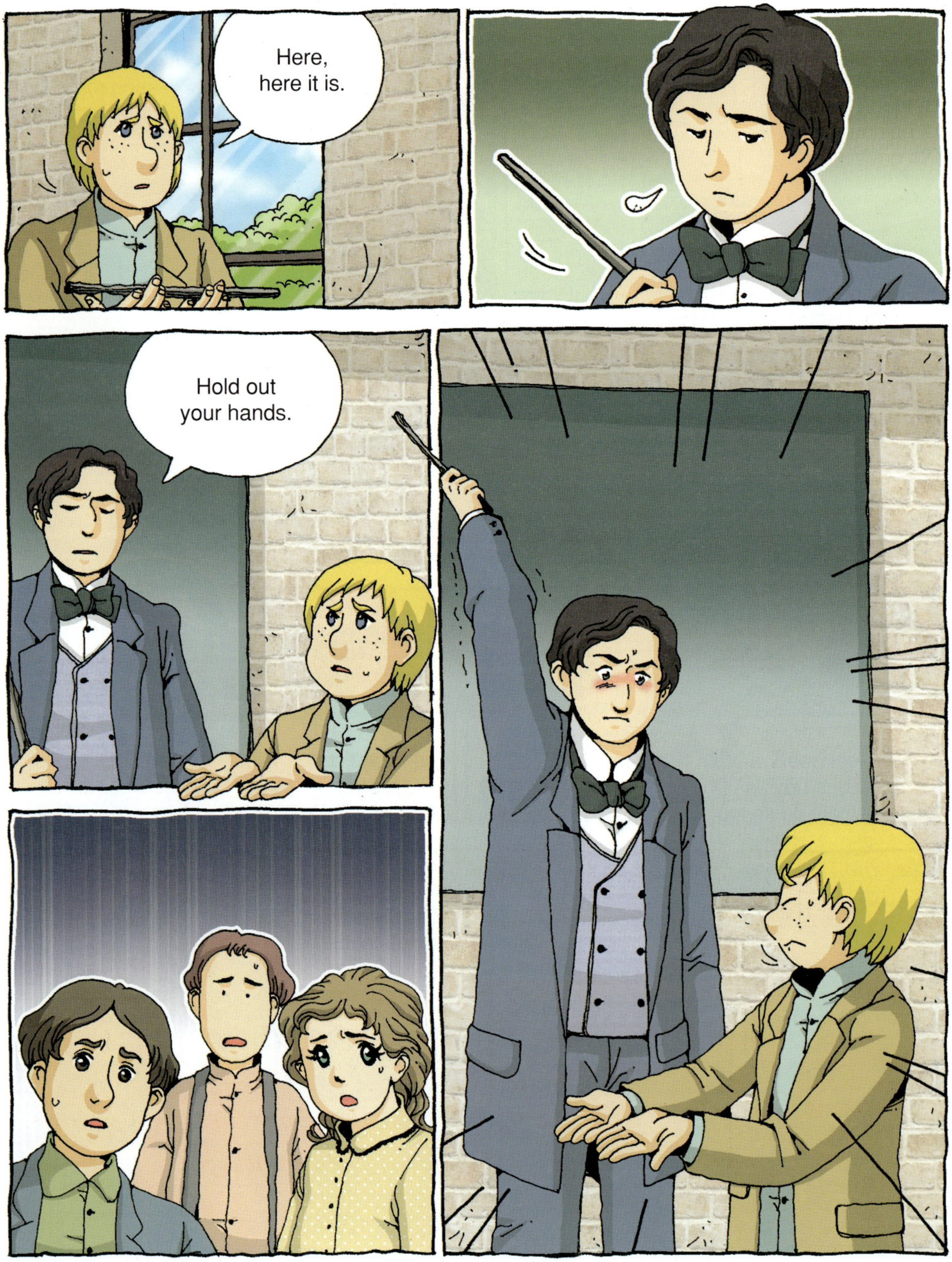

SLAP
Ow!

S-sir,
I'm sorry.

My goodness,
what have I done?

Are you
alright? I'm
sorry, Jack!

I won't do
it again.

Mr. Thoreau!
What are you doing?
That is not severe
enough.

No.

My conscience will not allow me to do this. If I must hit students in order to be a teacher, then I would rather quit.
Wh-what?
Henry was so mortified by the fact that he had actually hit a student. He ended up quitting his job as a result of this incident. He was following his conscience.

05 On the Concord River

Henry established a school together with his brother, John. The most fundamental teaching of this school was that it was "a school where students study on their own without corporal punishment."

A place where students learn to study on their own

Now, what kind of environment do birds need in order to live?

Close your books, for the answer is in nature. We're all going to go outside. Let's take a look in the woods.

In the woods?

Children,
look at this.

Oooh,
it's a bird!

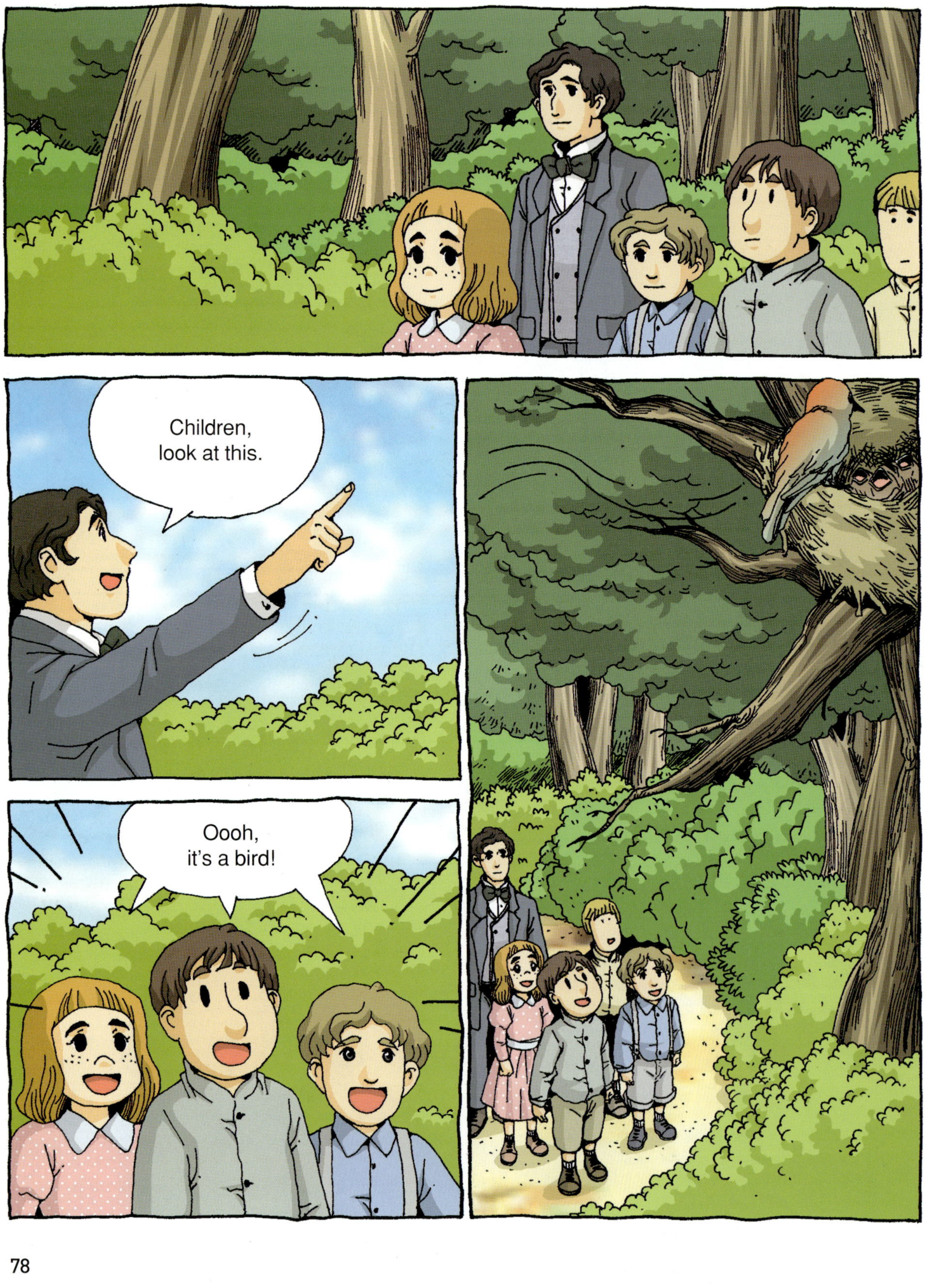

Did you see that? Did you see the bird going into its nest?
Yes. It's interesting that it lives in such a high place.
Now, shall we discuss what kind of environment a bird needs to live in?
It needs a nest.
It needs a tree to build the nest in.
That's right. You all are correct.
Mr. Thoreau, why is the bird flying back and forth?
It's looking for something to eat.

Then it must have to build its nest near a place with a lot of food.

Haha. That's true.

Mr. Thoreau, look at these pretty flowers! I want to take them home.

Oh, no! You must not disturb nature.

Why?

Do you want the birds living up there in the nest to die?

If you pick those flowers, then the insects that eat the sweet part of the flowers will starve and probably die. Then what do you think will happen to the birds that eat those insects?

It won't have anything to eat.

No.

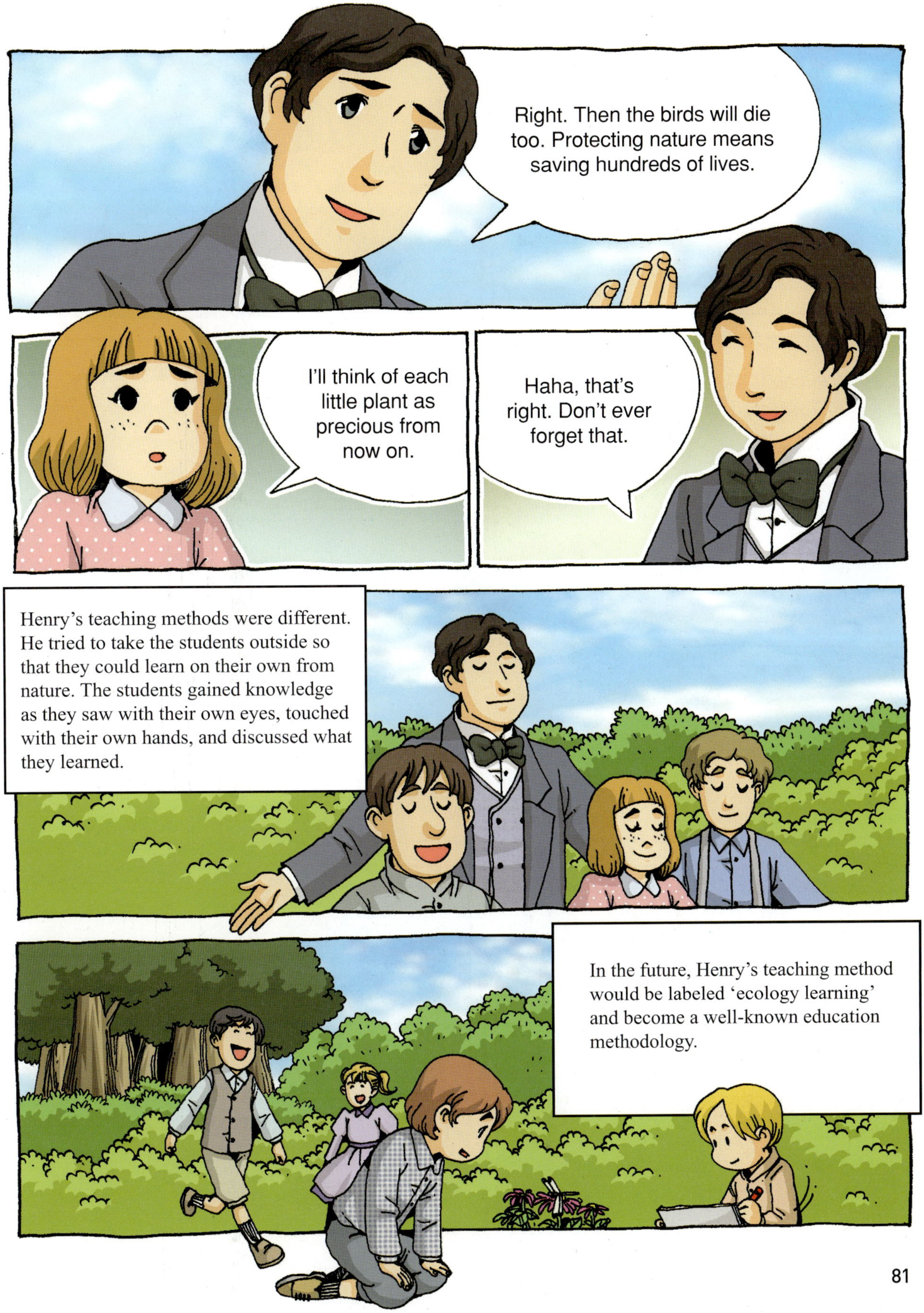

Henry's teaching methods were different. He tried to take the students outside so that they could learn on their own from nature. The students gained knowledge as they saw with their own eyes, touched with their own hands, and discussed what they learned.

In the future, Henry's teaching method would be labeled 'ecology learning' and become a well-known education methodology.

Track 37 ▶
Henry's school soon drew many people's interest. Parents would visit the school in order to observe his teaching methods for themselves.

How can I help you?
I want to send my children to this school so I want to see for myself what kind of school this is.
Well, you're just in time to see a class about to start in the classroom. Come this way.

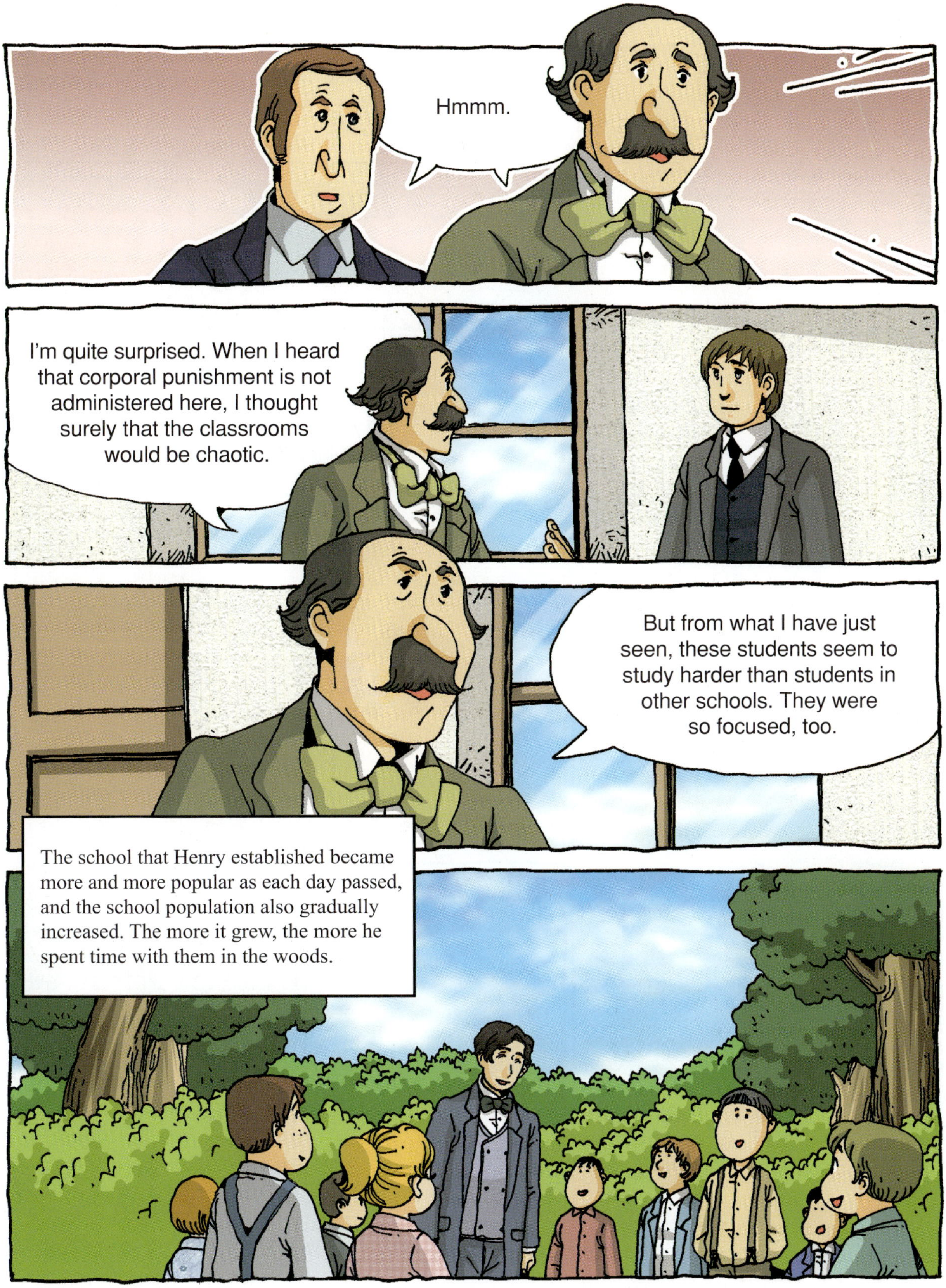

The school that Henry established became more and more popular as each day passed, and the school population also gradually increased. The more it grew, the more he spent time with them in the woods.

As Henry watched the children learning in nature, it made him long for his childhood days when he freely ran around and played.
John, do you want to go travel somewhere?
Why all of a sudden?
Let's go during the school vacation.
I bet there's something unusual about the travel you're thinking about.
Yup. I was thinking about sailing down the river and just drifting wherever the waters take us.

Sailing down the river, huh?
Yeah, and when it starts getting dark, we can tie the boat down and camp on the riverside.
When we're hungry, we can go fishing or eat fruit from the trees.
Hahaha! I'm getting excited just thinking about it. Let's go!
Henry and his brother, John, began their journey down the river in a sailboat. In the future, Henry gathered the records he made of this journey and published it as a book, called A Week on the Concord and Merrimack Rivers.

Hello there. Where are you two headed?
We're following the course of this river.
You're journeying down the river, huh? Haha, just like young people! Good luck to you!
You too, sir!

The Thoreau brothers met many people as they rowed down the river. They talked to boatsmen traveling to different places and were welcomed by children who lived on the riverside.
Those kids, they're trying to follow us, aren't they?
Yeah. We must be fascinating to them.
Yeah, yeah, nice to see you, too!

Should we try to go faster?
Sure!

Open the sail!

Wow, so refreshing!
I feel great!

Sigh, I'm hungry.
How can we fish for several hours and not catch a single fish?
Uh? I got a bite!
Good job, Henry! We can finally eat dinner!

The brothers journeyed down the river for two weeks. Before he went to sleep each night, Henry wrote down all of the day's events.

Aahhh. Living like this could be pretty romantic.

I wish we could quit teaching and live like this.

That's not a bad idea. I'd want to do that if it weren't for the kids waiting for us.

Yeah, you'd never be able to do it. You love those kids more than you love your own brother.

But one day, I want to live like this in nature.

After completing the two weeks of traveling, Henry treasured the feelings he experienced in nature and returned back to normal life. But then one day...

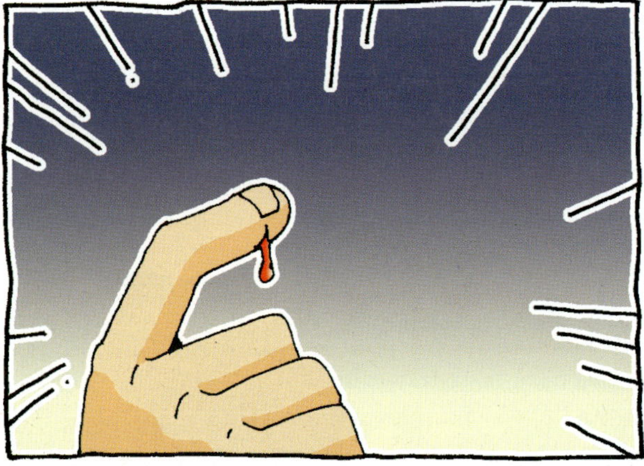

A little later, the small cut which didn't seem serious developed into lockjaw, and endangered John's life. Lockjaw is a dangerous disease that forms when a bacteria enters the body through a wound, and causes death in a short period of time.

Not much time passed before John passed away. Henry couldn't believe the sudden death of his brother.
John, are you still sleeping?
Jo-John...

John, wake up!
John!

Henry, let's let
him go now.

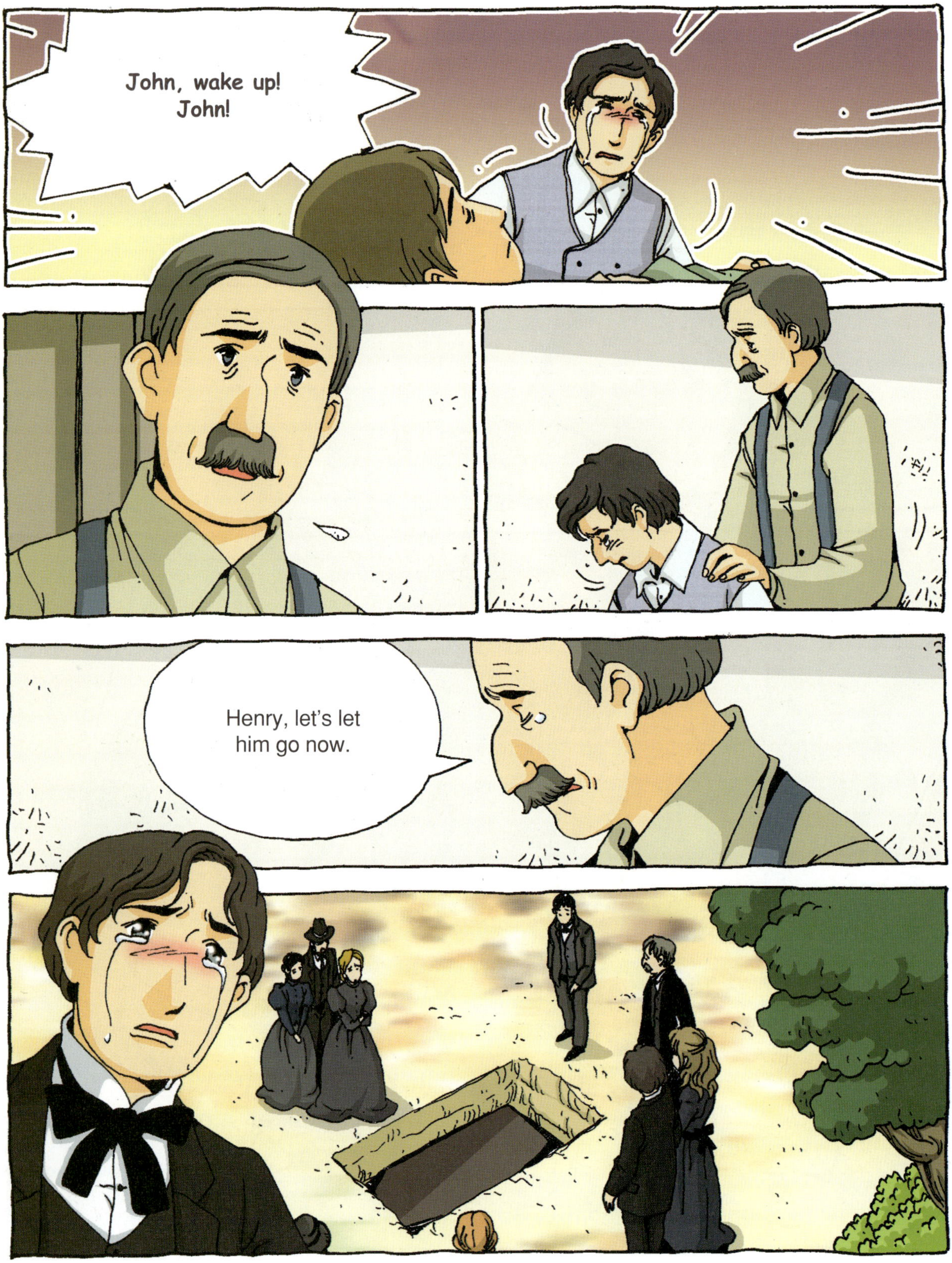

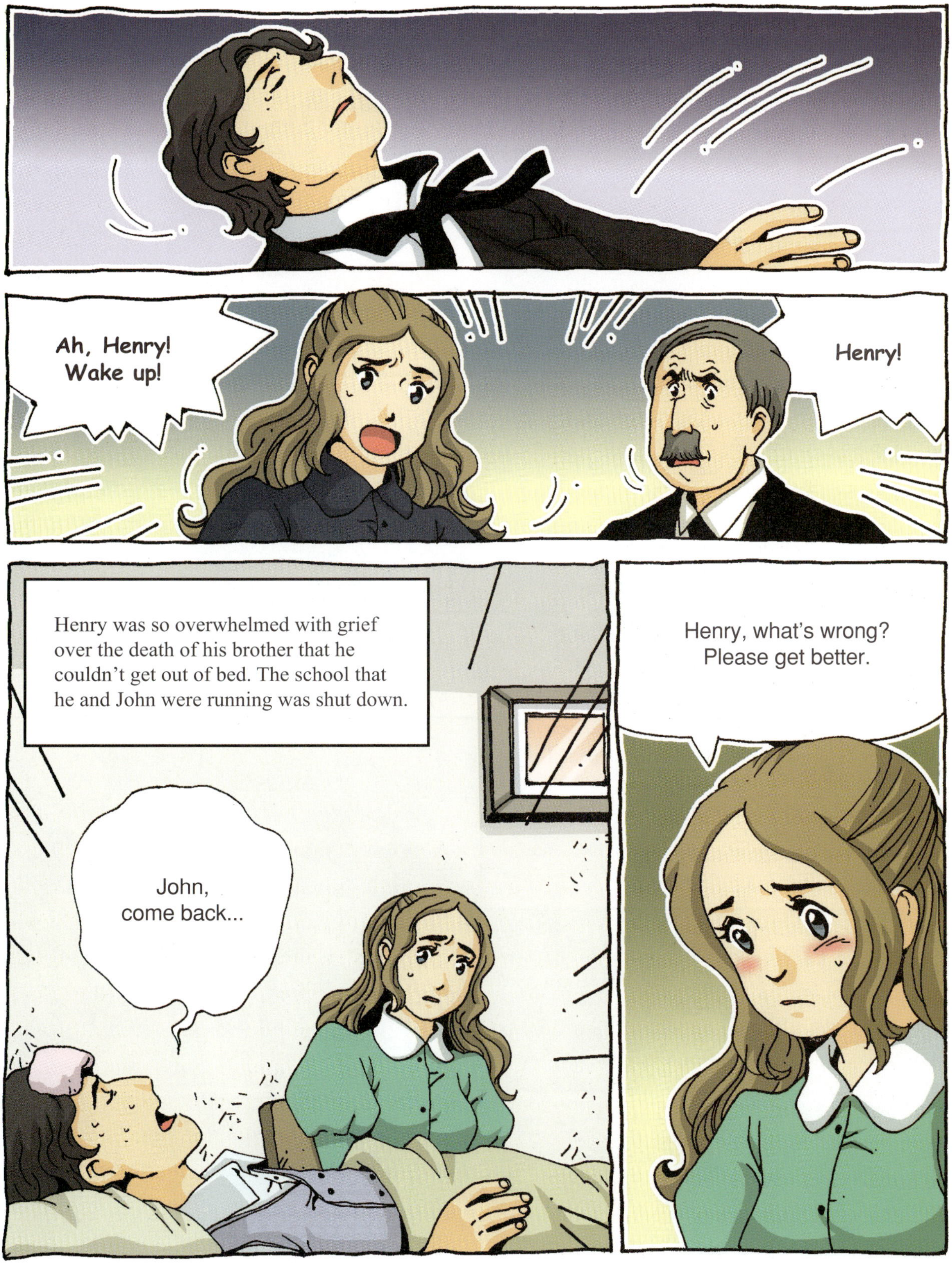

Henry was so overwhelmed with grief over the death of his brother that he couldn't get out of bed. The school that he and John were running was shut down.

06 · To Walden Pond

It wasn't until the season had changed that Henry could gradually overcome his grief.

While he was working at his father's pencil factory, he would write in his spare time and send it to Emerson. Emerson, in turn, published Henry's writing in a transcendentalist magazine called *The Dial*.

The more he wrote, the more ambitious Henry became. Instead of writing short pieces for the magazine, he wanted to write a serious piece about himself.
I could probably write a great book if I wrote in a quiet, isolated place in the woods.

Henry met with Emerson to ask for some help.

Henry, it's been a long time. Have a seat here.

Mr. Emerson, I came because I have something I want to ask you.

I understand that you have some land on Walden Pond, in Concord.

Yes, there is a beautiful view there.
Could you let me use that land? I would like to stay there and do some writing.
I am thinking about building my own cabin, growing a garden, and living there for a while. Then I will write about this experience and publish it into a book.
That sounds fantastic! That is truly living with nature.
Then do I have your permission?
Of course.

After getting permission from Emerson, he started building a cabin that would be suitable for him to live in.

Henry chopped down the tree and cut it into smaller pieces with an axe.
Hey, what are you doing there?
I'm building a house.
A house? All by yourself? You're out of your mind.

People thought Henry was strange, but he paid no attention to them and worked hard on making his cabin.
Hmm, it's a little too small for me to lie down.

While he was building the cabin, he would go into town whenever he needed to buy more materials.
How much is this?

Henry, what are you going to do with all those nails?
I'm making a house.

You're making a house? All by yourself?

How's the construction going?
Good, as you can see.

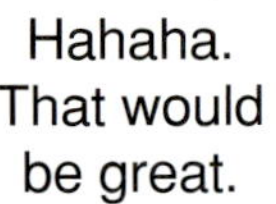

Henry's cabin was quite decent. In the final step of covering the cabin with planks and pasting on the lime, Emerson and the transcendentalist scholars came to help.

Occasionally he got help from his friends and family, but for the most part, Henry built his cabin entirely by himself.

Planks	$8.00
Secondhand planks used on roof and walls	$4.00
Lath strips*	$1.25
Secondhand glass windows, two	$2.43
Secondhand bricks, 1000	$4.00
Lime, two cans	$2.40
Lime paste	$0.31
Iron grate for fireplace	$0.15
Nails	$3.90
Hinges* and screws	$0.14
Bolt	$0.10
Chalk	$0.01
Material transportation	$1.40
Total	$28.09

*lath strips: Wood strips woven inside dirt walls in order to allow pasting.
*hinges: Metal pieces which allow doors to open and close.

28 dollars. This is about $1,000 in current dollar value. Henry was able to build himself a house with that small amount of money.
28 dollars... Hahaha. I built a house with less than the amount of one year of room and board at Harvard.

Are you doing okay living in your cabin in the woods, Henry?
Of course. Everything is quite satisfactory.
What brings you into town?
I want to buy potato and bean seeds to plant in my garden.

Oh, are you planning to raise your own crops and sustain yourself on them?
If it's possible.
So I just till the soil and plant the seeds. Is that all? When do I need to give the fertilizer?
No, I'll leave it to nature.

Henry started a garden next to his cabin and planted potatoes, beans, and corn. But he didn't use fertilizer even once and left his crops to grow naturally by themselves.

The first year of farming.
The garden became full with crops grown completely organically.

My goodness!
You harvested
all this?

Yes.

Sir, how much
can I get for
this much?

Let's see...

You should be able to
get at least $23.

Haha. Do you
remember how much
I paid for the seeds?

Well, how much
was it now?

14 dollars and 72 cents.
Then you've made about $8 in profit!
Thoreau earned $23.44 selling the crops he harvested from his vegetable garden. Out of that amount, about $4.50 was earned from crops that grew on land outside the garden on their own.
I did a pretty decent job farming, even if I don't take into consideration the portion I ate. I didn't buy a large plow or use a cow to plow the field. It is obvious that if I had a cow, I wouldn't have been able to do anything else but take care of the cow.
Man can live an abundantly happy life without exerting force on an animal or another human being if he gets rid of his greed. I have no problem living with my current income and expenditures.

Actually, the amount that Henry earned from selling the crops he grew was far too small to make a living. When he needed money to buy cheese or milk or a winter coat, he would go into town and work for some wages.

Henry, you have some fine craftsman skills.

After building a house all by myself, this is a piece of cake. If you have any other work for me, call me anytime.

Eight months had quickly passed since Henry started living in his cabin at Walden Pond.

Henry, are you here?

Come in, Mr. Emerson.

I was curious to see how you were doing here. And I haven't seen you in quite a while.
Just a minute. I was just in the middle of feeding a mouse some cheese.
A mouse?
Haha. You've made a friend.
In the morning, I have another friend that wakes me up with a menacing howl.
Menacing howl?

Income

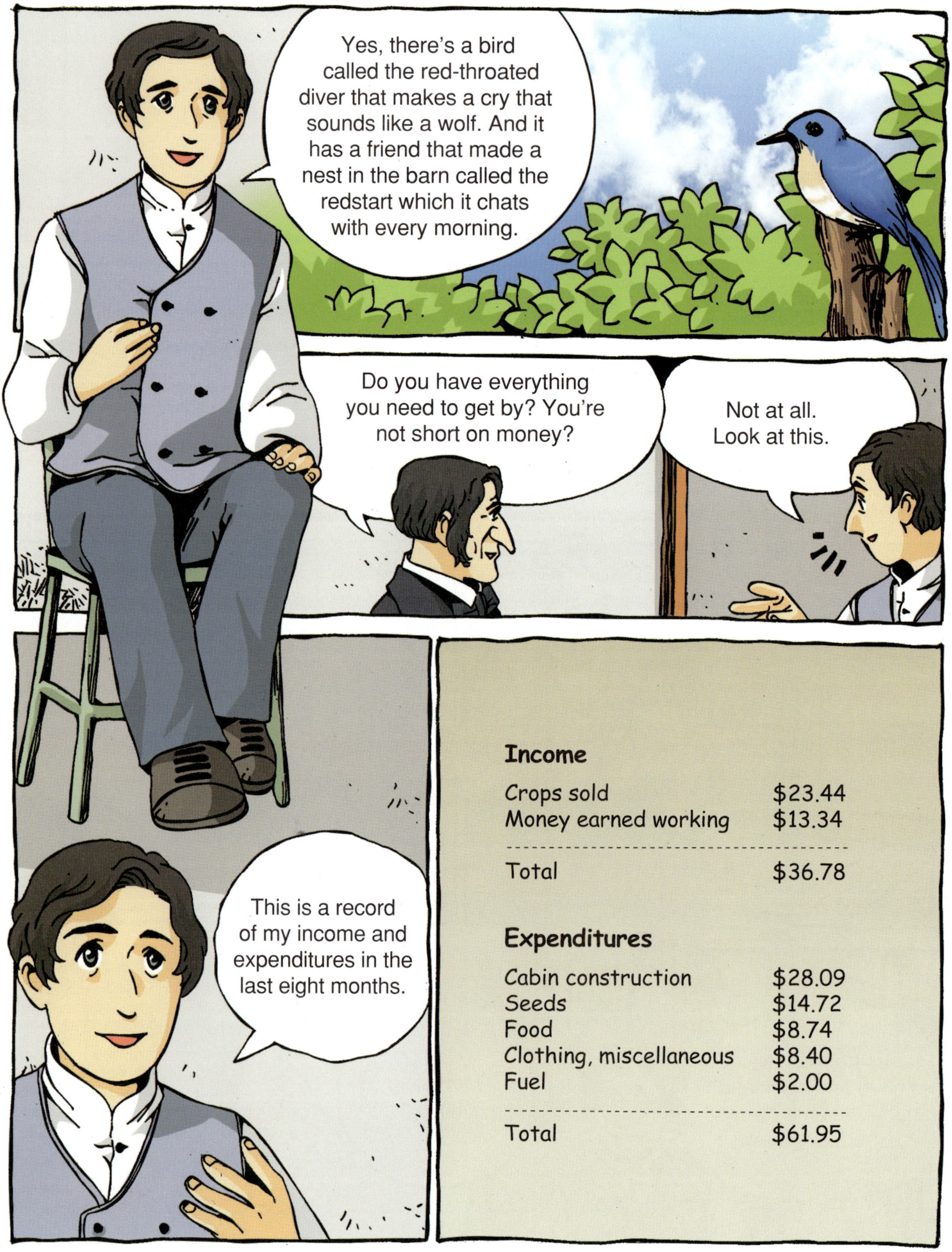

Crops sold	$23.44
Money earned working	$13.34
Total	$36.78

Expenditures

Cabin construction	$28.09
Seeds	$14.72
Food	$8.74
Clothing, miscellaneous	$8.40
Fuel	$2.00
Total	$61.95

Besides the cost of the construction of the cabin, Henry basically only spent $4 a month in expenses.

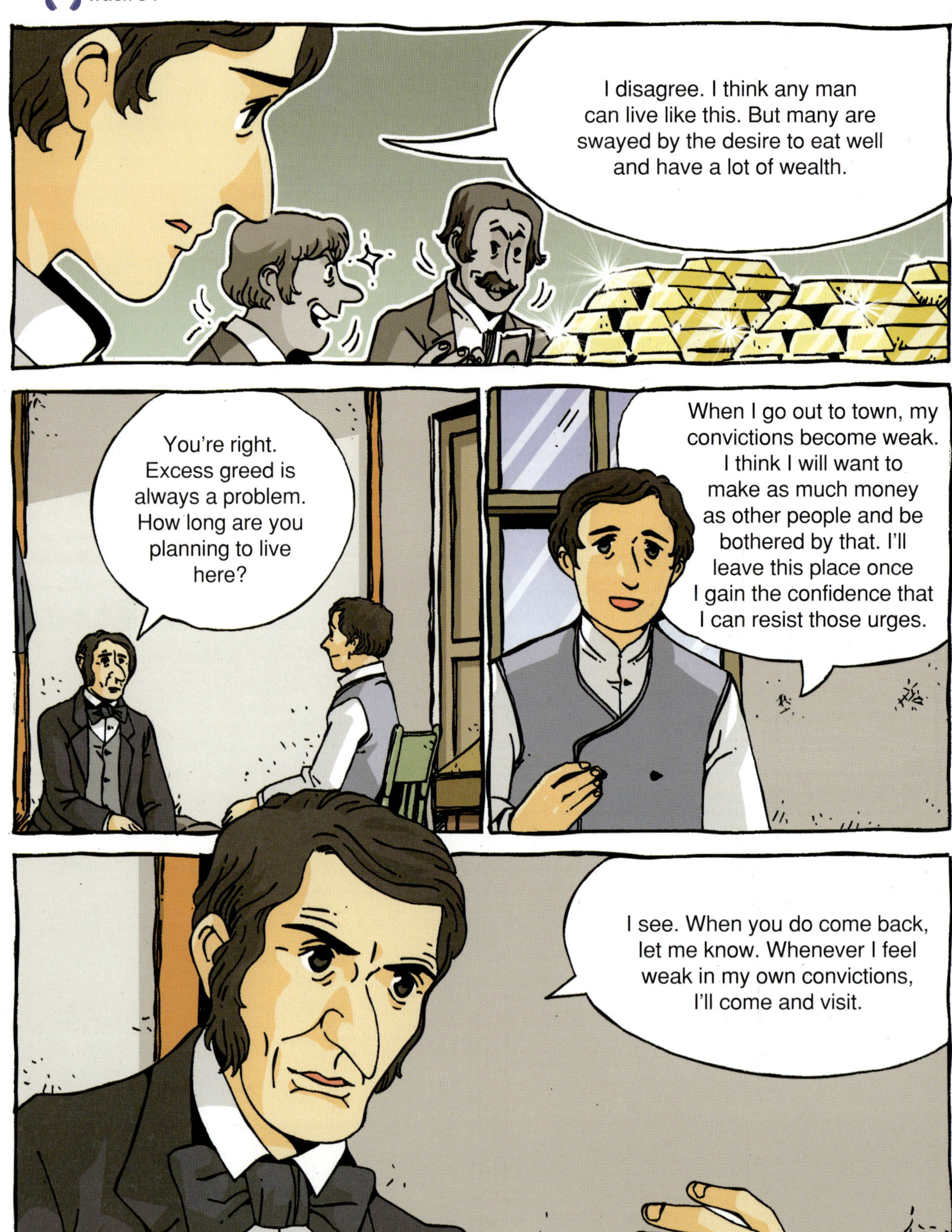

I disagree. I think any man can live like this. But many are swayed by the desire to eat well and have a lot of wealth.
You're right. Excess greed is always a problem. How long are you planning to live here?
When I go out to town, my convictions become weak. I think I will want to make as much money as other people and be bothered by that. I'll leave this place once I gain the confidence that I can resist those urges.
I see. When you do come back, let me know. Whenever I feel weak in my own convictions, I'll come and visit.

Once in a while, his friends and family came to visit, but for the most part, Henry spent most of his time alone. After spending time with the animals and plants in his surroundings, when winter came, he would watch the white snow pile up outside the cabin and write.

Two years had passed since Henry started living at Walden Pond, and spring had come again.

There.
That should
do it...

I'm ready to
leave now.

07 •**Eternal Naturalist**

Henry returned to town after living in his cabin at Walden Pond for two years. He believed that he now had the strength to resist any worldly persuasion which might lead him away from his simple life.

Mr. Henry David Thoreau?
Yes?

I'm with the police. You are under arrest.
I have done nothing to warrant being arrested.

No, you have not paid the compulsory citizens tax for two years.

Tax?

*holding cell: A place to temporarily hold a person who has committed a minor crime.

The institution of slavery, war... I refuse to allow my taxes to support these unjust policies.
The reason Henry didn't pay his taxes was not because he lived alone in the woods. He didn't like the fact that the taxes he paid would be used where he didn't want them to be used.
Look here. Are you not a citizen of this country? Every citizen must pay his taxes.
Just as the government can punish its citizens, citizens have the right to reject a government which is doing wrong.

Henry wrote an essay called, *Civil Disobedience*, containing his thoughts on this issue. It includes his main premise, "Citizens have the right to reject a government's policies, and the government may not infringe on the freedom of its citizens."

Henry stayed true to his conscience and refused to pay the taxes. The amount that was overdue was paid by a generous citizen, and Henry was freed. The identity of the person who paid Henry's taxes is still unknown even today.

Henry was more disappointed than thankful to the anonymous person.

Now that Henry had the freedom to do what he wanted, he wrote a book about his journey with his brother, John, called A Week on the Concord and Merrimack Rivers. But it didn't sell as well as he thought it would.
What is this, Henry?
My book. They weren't selling, so I bought them all.
You bought your own books?
Can you do that?
What's wrong with that? I can just keep them and give them to people who want them later.
Yup.

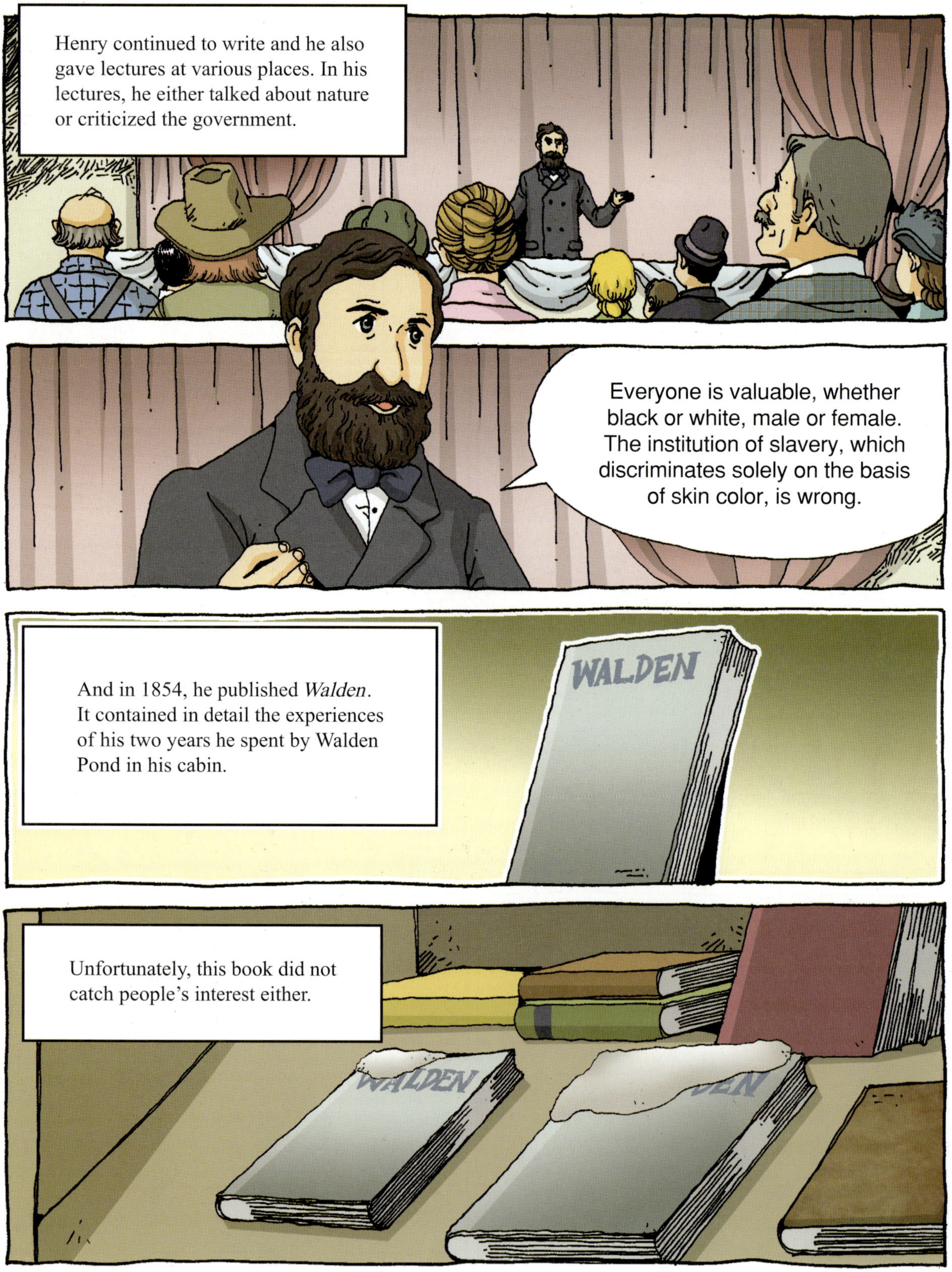

Henry continued to write and he also gave lectures at various places. In his lectures, he either talked about nature or criticized the government.

Everyone is valuable, whether black or white, male or female. The institution of slavery, which discriminates solely on the basis of skin color, is wrong.

And in 1854, he published *Walden*. It contained in detail the experiences of his two years he spent by Walden Pond in his cabin.

Unfortunately, this book did not catch people's interest either.

Even after he returned home, Henry continued to travel along the river and in the woods, and live in the midst of nature. Then one day...
Cough! Cough!
Cough! Cough! Ergh!

Henry went to the doctor to get a diagnosis, sensing something was wrong with his health.
Sophia, could I please speak with you?
Yes.
Doctor, is the cold quite serious?
Henry's illness was tuberculosis. At the time, tuberculosis was a formidable disease which took people's lives.
He has tuberculosis.
What?

I think you should prepare for the inevitable.
It-it can't be. How could Henry...
Henry...
It must not be good news.
No, he just said your cold was serious.
Sophia, it's alright. I'm not afraid of anything.

Everyone dies eventually. We were created from nature so we will return to nature.
But...
Sophia, after the winter passes, the spring comes, doesn't it?
When spring comes, leaves spring up from dry twigs and flower buds appear. The animals we didn't see all winter come out and stretch; the birds gather under the sun and sing.
That's how nature continues on and on.
Yes.
When I return to nature, I'll be able to live there forever. So don't grieve.

Henry's health continued to worsen as days passed. He couldn't eat or speak properly.

Look around carefully, Henry.
There! There's something to hunt!
Henry, that's a moose!
Yeah! I'll catch it this time.

Moose...
Indian...
Henry passed away
at the young age of 44.
Henry!

Henry's book, *Walden*, began to gain fame after he died, and 150 years later, it is still being read worldwide.

As civilization has advanced and society has become more complicated, people now live a much more comfortable life than in the past. However, new problems have also arisen.

The environment has become polluted, the ecosystem has been destroyed, and the warmth of the human heart has disappeared. People these days carelessly use the resources available to them, and live busy lives with little time for relaxation.

In this context, the ideas that Henry put forth as he pursued a life in harmony with nature are now drawing attention once more.

Pursuing life which preserves nature and finding contentment while living with the minimum necessities. Modern day people found peace of mind through Henry's book.

In addition, Henry's example of living out a simple life without greed and living with only the most essential necessities from nature is an important lesson to modern day people who constantly strive for bigger and better things. This kind of mindset allows them to be happy and thankful for every little thing in life.

Meanwhile, Emerson's family, who considered Henry a member of their family, made the area surrounding Henry's cabin at Walden Pond into a park. They wanted people who wanted to learn about Henry's life to be able to come and visit.

Henry David Thoreau.
He was a man of nature and a man of freedom.

He loved nature just as it was and believed that that was its most beautiful state. He wished to live as a part of nature.

Henry David Thoreau, the philosopher of simplicity who spoke of how the more one possessed, the stronger one's greed and the farther from happiness one became. Being one with nature even today, he smiles down on those who come to visit his Walden cabin.

Word Search

● Find the words which are hidden horizontally, vertically and diagonally.

```
A M Z G Q M Z G Q M Z G Q Q M Z G L M X
W S I N A E N T E O N H W W N A H O N O
E B W J A D I S C I P L I N E R I C B M
R V C A R D C K R V V K R R V C K K V M
E C T O Y S E N T C U L T T C D U J C E
V X E Q Y N E O Y X N Q Y Y X E N A X M
E Z V W U D I W C O E R C I O N J W Z W
A N A E I A E O L A E E E I A R A E A I
L S I R O S G C E S L R H O C G S R S T
P D C U P D H T R D I E O P O H T B D P
E F A Y H F U Y G T C Y V A N U Y I F L
S G S U S T I N Y R A G E I S G U T G R
T H S I D H M I D H L I R D T O I Y H U
P H I L O S O P H E R J F F R T J F J S
R K N P R H P O R T I O N A U E B G K I
H L A N H L E N H E E N H H C E N H L B
J Q T M J Q T A U T D O R I T Y M J B L
C O N T E N T M E N T Q L L I Y Q L U E
Z W R E B E N T Z W K F Z Z O U F T J R
X E M E X M R I N C P O S M N R E X N M
W R Q C T R Q C P R O P H T R Q C C R P
```

contentment	clergy	coercion	lockjaw
sway	construction	philosopher	discipline

Vocabulary

● Match each word to the correct meaning.

1. eternal	• 소박함
2. tranquility	• 어마어마한
3. pollute	• 영원한
4. ecosystem	• 평온
5. simplicity	• 생태계
6. formidable	• 오염시키다
7. transcendentalist	• 체벌
8. corporal punishment	• 수확
9. ecology	• 생태학
10. isolate	• 절약하는
11. harvest	• 격리하다
12. frugal	• 초월론자

Guess What?

● Guess what he said in the blank.

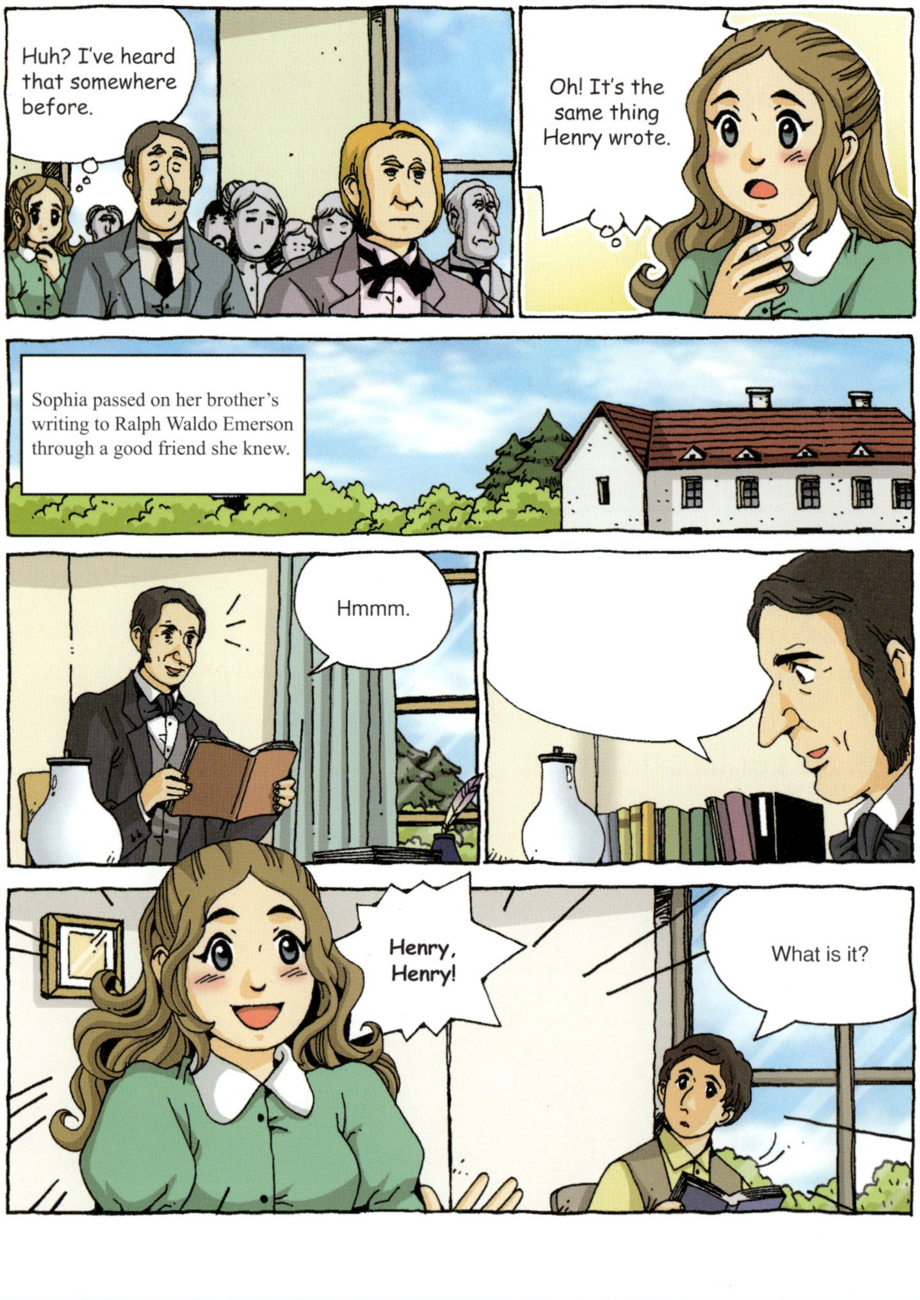

Cabin in the Woods

From 1845 to 1847, Henry David Thoreau lived in a small self-built cabin on the shore of Waldon Pond, Massachusetts. There he observed nature and recorded everything he saw, felt, and thought through the beauty and energy of nature in his poetic also scientific journals. Thanks to the life in the woods, in 1854, *Waldon*, his masterwork filled with nature's inspiration was published.

▲ Draw the beautiful natural surroundings around your cabin, and write about a day in the woods like Henry David Thoreau did at Waldon Pond.

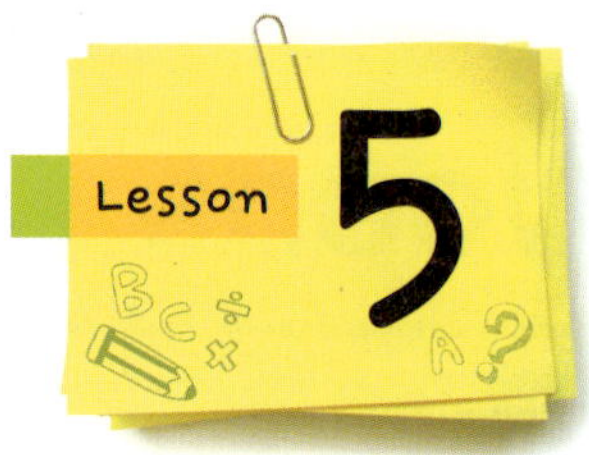

Lesson 5 Leaves

In *Walden*, Henry David Thoreau told us that nature is the outward sign of inward spirit, and interpretations on how people live. Even leaves are all different but sharing common ways to live sincere lives like humans do.

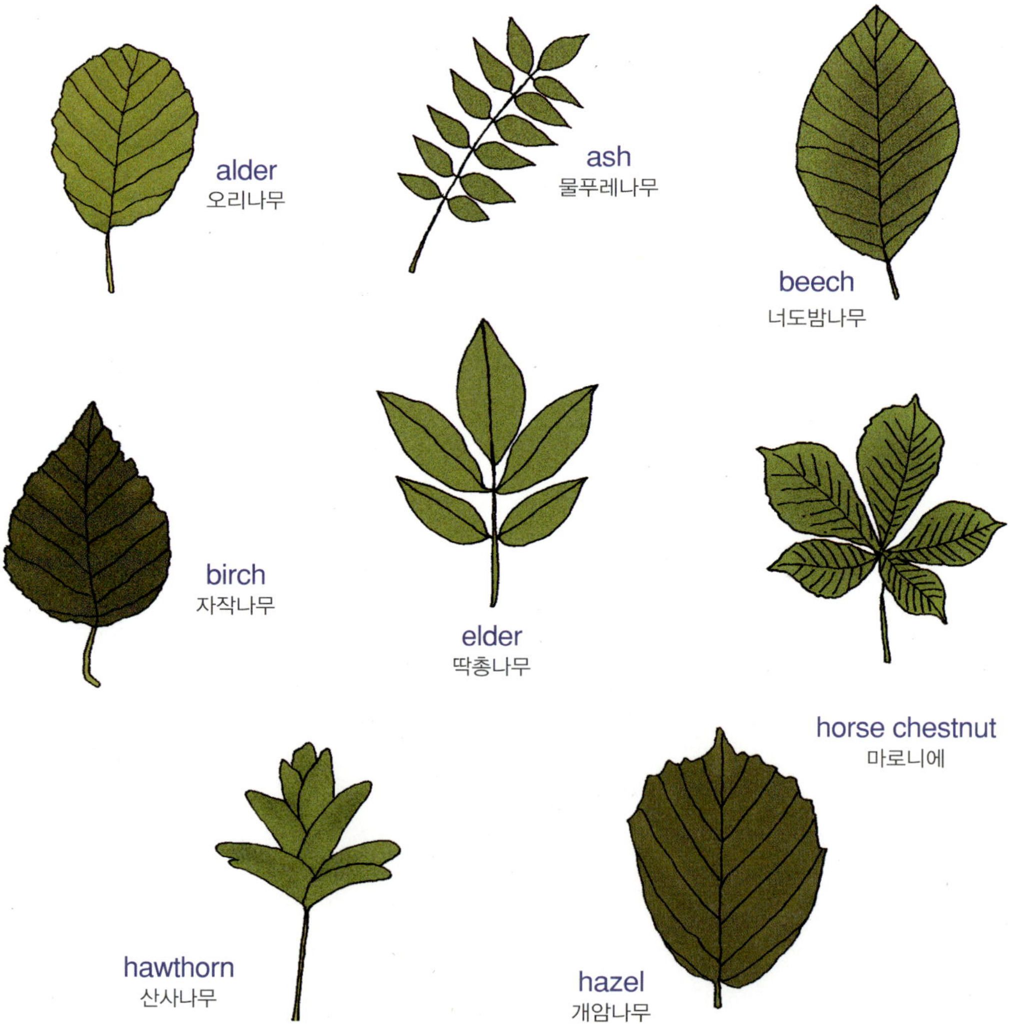

alder
오리나무
ash
물푸레나무
beech
너도밤나무
birch
자작나무
elder
딱총나무
horse chestnut
마로니에
hawthorn
산사나무
hazel
개암나무

● Draw the leaf you found in your garden or on the street.

1817년	7월 12일, 매사추세츠 주 콩코드에서 태어났습니다.
1821년 4세	가족이 보스턴으로 이주했습니다.
1823년 6세	다시 콩코드로 돌아와 콩코드 아카데미에 입학하였습니다.
1827년 10세	최초의 에세이 '계절'을 썼습니다.
1833년 16세	하버드 대학교에 입학하였습니다.
1837년 20세	에머슨을 만납니다. 선생님으로 일하던 중 학생 체벌을 거부하고 스스로 교직을 그만둡니다.
1839년 22세	형 존과 함께 사설 학교를 운영합니다. 형 존과 함께 강줄기를 따라 여행을 합니다.
1842년 25세	형 존이 파상풍으로 사망합니다.
1845년 28세	월든 호숫가에 오두막을 짓고 살기 시작합니다. 『콩코드 강과 메리맥 강의 일주일』을 집필하기 시작합니다.

1847년 30세   월든 호수에서 나왔습니다.

1848년 31세   세금 납부 거부로 감옥에 갇혔던 경험을 바탕으로
               '정부와의 관계에서 개인의 권리와 의무'에 대한 강연을 합니다.

1849년 32세   『콩코드 강과 메리맥 강의 일주일』을 출판합니다.

1853년 36세   『콩코드 강과 메리맥 강의 일주일』 초판 1000부 중
               팔리지 않은 706부를 구입합니다.

1854년 37세   월든 호숫가에서 지낸 경험을 바탕으로 쓴 책 『월든』이 출간됩니다.

1860년 43세   모나드녹 산에서 5일간 야영합니다. 이것이 소로의 마지막 야영입니다.

1861년 44세   의사의 권유로 휴양을 위해 미네소타로 갑니다.
               여동생 소피아가 소로의 원고를 정리해 줍니다.

1862년 45세   『산책』을 발표합니다.
               5월 6일, 콩코드에서 생을 마감합니다.

who? 01	Barack Obama	978-89-6370-514-9
who? 02	Charles Darwin	978-89-6370-515-6
who? 03	Bill Gates	978-89-6370-516-3
who? 04	Hillary Clinton	978-89-6370-517-0
who? 05	Stephen Hawking	978-89-6370-518-7
who? 06	Oprah Winfrey	978-89-6370-519-4
who? 07	Steven Spielberg	978-89-6370-520-0
who? 08	Thomas Edison	978-89-6370-521-7
who? 09	Abraham Lincoln	978-89-6370-522-4
who? 10	Martin Luther King, Jr.	978-89-6370-523-1
who? 11	Louis Braille	978-89-6370-439-5
who? 12	Albert Einstein	978-89-6370-440-1
who? 13	Jane Goodall	978-89-6370-441-8
who? 14	Walt Disney	978-89-6370-442-5
who? 15	Winston Churchill	978-89-6370-443-2
who? 16	Warren Buffett	978-89-6370-444-9
who? 17	Nelson Mandela	978-89-6370-445-6
who? 18	Steve Jobs	978-89-6370-446-3
who? 19	J. K. Rowling	978-89-6370-447-0
who? 20	Jean-Henri Fabre	978-89-6370-448-7
who? 21	Vincent van Gogh	978-89-6370-449-4
who? 22	Marie Curie	978-89-6370-450-0
who? 23	Henry David Thoreau	978-89-6370-451-7
who? 24	Andrew Carnegie	978-89-6370-452-4
who? 25	Coco Chanel	978-89-6370-453-1
who? 26	Charlie Chaplin	978-89-6370-454-8
who? 27	Ho Chi Minh	978-89-6370-455-5
who? 28	Ludwig van Beethoven	978-89-6370-456-2
who? 29	Mao Zedong	978-89-6370-457-9
who? 30	Kim Dae-jung	978-89-6370-458-6